Lambs Farm

RICK KOGAN | MARK JOSEPH

Lambs Farm

Where People Grow

Helping people with developmental disabilities lead productive,
happy lives and connecting with the human spirit in us all.

Contemporary Photography: © 2011 Mark Joseph Photography, Inc.
www.markjosephphoto.com

Book Design: Bob Feie
Printing: Quad/Graphics, Burlington, Wisconsin

Printed in the United States of America.

THIS BOOK IS DEDICATED TO BOB TERESE AND CORINNE OWEN, WHOSE LOVE AND COMPASSION FOR THEIR "YOUNG PEOPLE" SPARKED A SIMPLE YET GLORIOUS IDEA, AND TO ALL THE FAMILIES AND SUPPORTERS WHOSE FORESIGHT HELPED BRING THAT IDEA TO LIFE.

"They were so excited, it made me want to cry."

FOREWORD

I grew up in Berwyn, and I vaguely remember a young boy who lived a few houses down from me. He never went to school. He stayed in his house most of the time. His name was Dennis, I remember that. And I remember my mother telling me that Dennis was "slow."

"You should feel sorry for him," she added.

As I recall, much to my shame today, I tried my best to avoid him.

That was my only experience, if you can even call it that, with someone who had what I now understand to be a developmental disability until I joined the Board of Directors of Lambs Farm in 1992.

I had previously been asked to join many other boards, but I turned down those offers because they seemed to me to be merely ceremonial positions. What interested me most about joining the Lambs Farm board—I said yes enthusiastically— was that it would give me the opportunity to actually meet the people I would be serving.

As with many remarkable things in history, Lambs Farm started in 1961 with a simple idea: *There must be more for people with developmental disabilities than is being offered.* That idea, of course, was formed out of the need of those we now serve, by the compassion of our co-founders, and by the hope and energy of families with nowhere to turn. It grew through enormous hard work, patience, and sacrifice.

"Above all, be patient. These young people have faced lives few of us can imagine. If you do become discouraged and frustrated, just think for a moment of the discouragement and frustration they must be feeling."—Bob Terese

No one could have envisioned what that idea would eventually mean to hundreds of people with developmental disabilities who today are living happy, productive lives. Harder and more painful to imagine is what life would have been like for them had that idea never been born.

When I joined the Lambs Farm Board of Directors and for sometime thereafter, I thought that co-founders Bob Terese and Corinne Owen were a married couple. I was certain that was the case. If they had separate families of their own, I reasoned, how could they possibly devote the essence of their entire beings to a cause that, although very worthwhile, held no personal connection to their lives? I was wrong, of course.

During my early years at Lambs Farm, Bob and Corinne would occasionally attend board meetings. Despite the fact that it was more than three decades since they had created Lambs, I was deeply impressed to hear them speak about their continued activities and ongoing fight for the people for whom they had already done so much. Having later met their families, it became apparent that their devotion had weaved itself throughout the generations that followed them.

Once in a while, board members were invited to have dinner at one of the residences. I always jumped at the opportunity to spend some time with the Participants, and the experience was always interesting and enlightening and fun. They would all meet me at the door and start talking to me, all at the same time. We would sit down to dinner, and I would be taken by how genuinely interested they were in me, asking nonstop questions:

Who was I? What did I do? Where did I live? Was I married? Did I have children?

Sometimes I brought desserts. One evening I brought caps with my company's logo—Brunswick—on them. They were so excited, it made me want to cry. Instead, I became more determined to spend as much time as I could with my new friends to better understand Lambs Farm.

When I became President of Lambs Farm in 2001, I knew many of the Participants, and had become familiar with the operation. At first I was taken by the contrasts in what I was experiencing, from the complexities required of human services agencies with the multitude of regulations from every state and federal agency imaginable, to the unreliability of the funding necessary to assure compliance with them, to the almost joyful simplicity with which the Participants went about their daily lives. Today, the regulations are simply part of daily routine. Unfortunately, the funding has become even less reliable. And the Participants are their own unique puzzles that I spend a great deal of my time trying to solve.

Now, 50 years since its founding, Lambs Farm is known all over the country and in many parts of the world. So many people have come and gone, all in some way leaving their mark, from our co-founders, to the determined families who helped start it all and those who worked to keep it going through the years, to those who served on the Board of Directors, to our dedicated staff, to our donors and volunteers, and to those who have supported our businesses. An eclectic group, to be sure, but one with a common bond forged from the shared belief in our mission.

> **"At Lambs Farm, administrators and Participants share responsibilities through love. We talk to each other as friends, and that means a regard for feelings."—Corinne Owen**

Lambs Farm has changed the lives of hundreds of people and their families. These are people who might never have otherwise had the opportunities to learn skills, to have jobs, to be as independent as possible if it weren't for the shared vision—the *idea*—of Bob Terese and Corinne Owen. The men and women we serve take what life has dealt them in stride, always wanting to learn more, do more, experience more, and accomplish more. As individuals, they know who they are, and they work diligently just to prove to themselves that they can do better, all the while hoping that others will treat them with the respect and dignity they deserve. They have grown beyond anyone's imagination, living lives that are full, happy, and most important, their own.

I, too, have grown and have come to understand what motivated our co-founders and the tenacity they possessed to forge ahead despite all manner of obstacles. Throughout our history, the struggles have remained. The government funding we receive pays only for life's most basic needs. Those programs that are essential to the quality of Partcipants' lives—social/recreational activities, nutritional/fitness support, dietary and behavioral services—do not even qualify for funding, leaving us to find financial support for them elsewhere. So, despite all of the progress that has been made, a half century later we are still fighting to survive.

It is an unbelievable experience and an ongoing pleasure to be friend, confidant, teacher, even pseudo-mother to a group of remarkable adults whose emotional age is typically akin to adolescence. Working to make life better for them has been the most gratifying and rewarding endeavor of my life. Although

I have never had children of my own, I now like to think that I have nearly 250. Sharing a piece of their lives inspires me to be a better person and makes me wish I had been smart or sensitive enough to get to know Dennis better way back when.

This year we are celebrating the 50th Anniversary of Lambs Farm. Much has changed over those 50 years because our co-founders had an *idea*. We wanted to create a book that pays tribute to them, celebrates the tremendous progress that has been made as a result of that idea, and helps perpetuate it into the future. The Lambs Farm story has touched my life, and I hope it will touch yours as well.

DIANNE YACONETTI
PRESIDENT AND CHIEF EXECUTIVE OFFICER

A young Rick Kogan and the infamous "Charlie"

CHARLIE

His name was Charlie and he was a schnauzer and we picked him out and picked him up at the Lambs Pet Shop, a small but jam-packed store at 913 North State Street on the Near North Side of Chicago, on an icy December morning in 1962.

He immediately became part of our family. My father, the author and newspaperman Herman Kogan, was particularly fond of him. On April 20, 1963 he wrote about Charlie in his weekly column in the Panorama section of the *Chicago Daily News.* He was smitten with "the very first dog I have ever owned in nearly a half century of otherwise adventurous living."

Writing tenderly, he went on: "Charlie whines charmingly at all lady dogs, at the grocery delivery boy, at the newspaper boy, at green taxicabs, at the lady who comes to clean on Wednesday, at Lou Mariano because he called him Dirty Charlie in his *North Loop News* column, at the alarm clock, at the old-fashioned horse-drawn carriage that has joined the sightseeing bus in the onslaught against our neighborhood."

In this column he described the Lambs Pet Shop as a "wonderful establishment where you can also buy other kinds of puppies or a monkey, macaw, deodorized skunk, raccoon, talking myna bird, tropical fish, canary, rooster, guppy, rhinestone collar and plainer ones, dog biscuits, fish food, innumerable other items from ceramic vases to four-color cards."

Charlie was never otherwise noted in the hundreds of stories or the two fine books that have been written about The Lambs since its founding in 1961. But in thinking about Charlie and

We cannot stress enough how vitally important it is to not talk down to our young people. They may lack intelligence, but they do not lack feelings.

*Bob and Corinne
at the opening of the
Lambs Pet Shop.*

The Lambs now, these 50 years later, and knowing that seven of the young people who worked in that pet store are alive and well, and remembering how that little dog enriched our family's life, I think about how The Lambs has enriched and empowered the lives of so many people and marvel that it continues to do so today.

My mother, Marilew, was fond of Charlie too and of the more contentious schnauzer we named Dufo and bought at Lambs the following year. But her attentions were also focused on the two people who ran the store, Bob Terese and Corinne Owen, and the young people who worked there. Whenever she went to the store to buy dog food or a new collar or a fresh chew toy she would bring me and my younger brother Mark with her and she would say, "Now, I want you boys to talk to the people working in the store. I want you to be nice to them and get to know them. They are not like any people you know. They are special people."

Not yet in our teens, we didn't really know what she meant. But we were nice to the people in the store and they were nice to us. We did try to get to know them, as much as we could in the short time we were in the store, getting our dogs' necessities and treats, and watching our mother in animated conversation with Bob and Corinne.

The people in the store did not seem all that different from other people we knew. They did not seem special. They just seemed happier than most of the people we knew.

Don't ask a developmentally disabled
person a question unless you are prepared
for an honest answer.

Participants assist customers at Lambs Pet Shop.

In treating our young people as individuals, we and the staff always have to take into account the differences in their characters and backgrounds— they aren't just a workforce, they are people.

The store—once called by another newspaper columnist "the heartwarmingest spot in town"—is long gone. It closed in September 1969, and where it stood now stands the sumptuous Elysian hotel/condominium complex. But I think about that store and I can hear the echoes, the yapping and squawking. I can almost see that old store, and the smiling faces.

Life is a series of memories, and in those memories there are lessons. We all learn, with time, that life is not fair. But we also can learn that in understanding others—those others who by color, race, religion, or genetics did not get a fair and full shot at all life has to offer—we can come to understand ourselves.

Thousands of people have shaped and shared this half century of Lambs history, all of it based solidly on the shared vision of its two founders, that pair of seat-of-the-pants pioneers, Bob and Corinne. From vastly different backgrounds, they were drawn together by the shared notion, controversial and even radical at the time, that it was possible to integrate "mentally retarded" people into everyday society. Those people are now referred to as developmentally disabled, and the Bob/Corinne approach is now called mainstreaming. And their mission continues.

It is sometimes easy to take for granted the opportunity that The Lambs gives to those in its care—to grab life, to grow. What is a bit harder to realize is the chance it also has given the rest of us—by luck, or purpose, or just because a little boy wanted a puppy—to grow.

"It's this quiet affection, this trust and faith in other people, that we have always found particularly appealing in the Lambs," Bob Terese wrote in 1970. "These people are really a blessing. All they want is love—the love that demonstrates care, concern, interest. In return, they will give you far more love than any normal child."

BOB

Bob Terese was Chicago born and bred, the son of Angela and Joseph Terese, who owned a grocery store in the vibrant Austin neighborhood on the city's West Side. A few months after graduating from high school, Bob enlisted in the U.S. Navy and within months was in the middle of World War II in the Pacific. He was assigned to a cargo ship that also carried troops and so was witness to the bloody battles of Iwo Jima and Okinawa.

He returned to Chicago and enrolled at DePaul University, leaving three years later a few courses short of a degree in physical education. By 1950 he was married to Mary Ruth Miller, whom he had met on a blind date, and they were starting a family that would soon include two children, Michael and Carol. But he was otherwise aimless, drifting through a series of jobs before landing with the Milwaukee Road railroad as a fireman-engineer.

Bob worked the midnight to 8 a.m. shift, a schedule that allowed him time to rehab the old home he had purchased. It also gave him ample time to worry about his future, to search for a career. He toyed with the idea of selling insurance. He applied for a job at a gas station.

Nothing panned out. But he was offered a job driving a bus for the Bonaparte School in the western suburbs. He took it, and on a September morning in 1957, he got what he later called his "first real view of the mentally retarded." He was not prepared for it.

"The kids began smiling at me, and I began to see them as individuals."

Bob Terese saw his professional growth at Bonaparte School as conceptually akin to the experience of the visitors, especially church and senior citizen groups, at Lambs Farm. "At first, they're reluctant. But they come to avail themselves of our dining room; they visit the stores. Our Lambs meet them and show them around. They leave excited about what they've seen. Soon all they will see is a person."

Years later, in his fine book *The Lambs of Libertyville,* author Tim Unsworth described Bob as "ordinary-looking as a post office clerk," a person who cares "little about appearance or pedigrees." But he did. Bob wrote in his own book, *A Flock of Lambs,* that he "liked attractive things and people. The mentally retarded children of the Bonaparte School were not attractive." Before going to the school he "was the kind of person who would cross the street to avoid a mentally retarded person."

His first day of driving, he recalled, "was hell. The kids couldn't talk, and when a girl in the back of the bus let out a shriek the hair on the back of my neck stood straight up." He tried to quit after that first day but was persuaded to stick it out for a week. He did, and on his third day driving, he recalled, "The kids began

Bob Terese and
Corinne Owen open
the Lambs Pet Shop
at 913 N. State St.
in Chicago,
employing 12 men
and women with
mental retardation

The Lambs moves
to 51-acre farm near
Libertyville with
the help of Chicago
philanthropist
W. Clement Stone

smiling at me, and I began to see them as individuals instead as
some sort of mindless creatures."

This revelation prompted an immediate change in his attitude
and also proved a turning point in his life, for he soon approached
the school's principal with the suggestion that he initiate an
exercise program for the children. "I didn't push them," he
recalled. "But I did keep them going." And going, and going,
moving from simple efforts to group and team pursuits.

When winter restricted the exercise and athletics, Bob took
advantage of the school's stove and sink and began to teach some
of the children to cook, to make simple things like baked bean
casseroles and Jell-O. He was joined in these efforts by another
newcomer to the school, teacher Corinne Owen, who had
started there a few months earlier. Though she and Bob belonged
to Wheaton Baptist Church, they hadn't met each other until
shortly after she was hired at Bonaparte School.

1966   **1967**

The Lambs' first business, a fruit and vegtable stand, opens; the Pet Shop opens, housed in a turn-of-the-century dairy barn

The Shepherd Inn restaurant opens for Sunday brunch

Silkscreen shop opens

It is important to know how profound a part religion played in the lives of these two people. And though both of them believed that God's hand was evident in everything that eventually came from their fruitful collaboration—the pet shop and its name, its success, the farm, everything—they were never overbearing about their beliefs.

"They were not at all pushy about it," the *Chicago Tribune's* Margit Leavitt wrote in a 1972 article. "Bob and Corinne don't force the issue."

In his book, Unsworth noted that during his first meeting with Bob and Corinne he was struck by their "sincerity and their true belief. Their religion is not exclusive. It is a religion of love."

That may well have been, and there is ample evidence to prove it, but it was not love at first sight when Bob and Corinne first met in the fall of 1957. Corinne was a carefully organized person. In Bob's words, she "just seemed too methodical, too cold, too reserved for me." She, in turn, found Bob to be "irresponsible."

1968

After seeing the remarkable progress of The Lambs program, the rental agreement is waived and the Libertyville land is donated outright by W. Clement Stone

Grandma's Bakery opens, home of Lambs' world-famous butter cookies

1969

The Children's Farmyard and Petting Zoo opens

But as they worked together, they began to see and know and appreciate one another's strengths and passionate interest in the children. Together, they expanded the cooking efforts. Together, they taught the kids to silkscreen; they made and sold Christmas cards. They orchestrated a Christmas show, with the children singing and dancing "and tears streaming down parents' cheeks when they saw their children perform."

In the spring of 1958, Bob was hired as a full-time teacher for the coming school year. By that time he had come to realize, as he later put it, that "the qualities Corinne and I sensed in each other and at first mistrusted were exactly the ones that would make us into an effective working team."

1969

1972

The Lambs Country
Store opens, producer
of Lambs' jams, jellies
and hand-dipped
chocolates

Dr. Karl Menninger
receives the
Good Shepherd
Award

W. Clement Stone
receives the Good
Shepherd Award

Bob Terese with
Corinne Owen writes
"A Flock of Lambs,
A New Approach to
the Care of the
Mentally Retarded"

*When Dr. Karl Menninger, the late psychiatrist who headed the Menninger
Foundation in Topeka, Kansas, came to visit The Lambs, we took him around
and then asked him to see our written work. 'No,' he said, 'I see the people;
they're happy, productive. And I see the current of love here.'"*

Corinne liked to tell the young people that she knew she could never be President of the United States. "But that doesn't stop me from doing what I can do," she said. "I can be happy doing less than the President if I know I do it well."

CORINNE

Corinne Owen was born Corinne Boren in Greenville, a town at the western edge of Ohio most famous as the birthplace of Annie Oakley. Her parents were Hazel and Ezra Boren, he a farmer and she a farmer's daughter.

The family, which included younger sister Dorothy, moved to Chicago in the mid-1920s so that Ezra, taken with a call to the ministry, could attend classes at the Moody Bible Institute. They lived on the West Side where Corinne attended grammar school and high school. Her father worked as an elevator operator when not in class, and her mother was a waitress.

Corinne worked too, during the summers, at a hot dog stand, and some of the money she earned there helped pay her tuition to North Park College where she studied music. Before graduating with her degree, she began to teach piano at various schools in the city, charging one dollar per lesson.

She was a tiny thing, barely five feet tall and soft-spoken. She married Trevor Owen in 1938. He was also an elevator operator but became a manufacturer's representative as the couple began a family that would include two daughters, Bette and Doris, and a son, Victor. They all lived for a time in a house shared with Corinne's parents in south suburban Blue Island before moving to a home, built by Trevor from a plan he found in a magazine, in West Chicago.

She gave up teaching to raise the children, but when Victor entered school she became a part-time salesperson for the Child-craft reading program. She was a natural, eventually averaging a stunning seven sales for every 10 calls that she made. She also began to sell subscriptions to *Life* magazine. Her life was good and stayed that way for many years.

Eventually, Corinne grew tired of sales and was eager for new challenges. One came when she had a conversation with her friend Jean Adams, who told her about the work she had been doing with the children at the Bonaparte School. Jean told her about the various things the children were doing with the help of a school bus driver named Bob Terese, who had begun working with them between driving them to and from school. Jean told Corinne about the children being taught some basics in music.

"I could do that," Corinne said.

"That's what I wanted to hear," said Jean, who then told her friend that she would be leaving the school soon to have her third baby and asked if Corinne might be interested in taking her place.

Corinne was, even as she realized that she had never met a mentally disabled person before, except perhaps one boy to whom she taught music and who she suspected "might be a little slow."

On one of her first visits to the school, a boy named Bruce threw his arms around Corinne's neck and said, "I love you." Bob saw this and later recalled that he immediately sensed the "warmth of her personality." In very little time, he watched Corinne display "an extraordinary ability to understand the innermost

*Many politicians and dignitaries personally experienced the work of
Bob and Corinne, such as Governor Richard Ogilvie who visited Lambs Farm
in the late 1960s.*

1974   **1976**

Clinton Frank
receives the
Good Shepherd
Award

Mr. and Mrs. William
Grainger (Grainger
Foundation) donate
$200,000 to complete
construction of
the Dorm (residential
facility for 37 residents)

U.S. Senator
Charles Percy visits

problems of the retarded; she can always get down to where the trouble is and, by dint of patient love and understanding, soothe that trouble. She can endure ugliness and temper tantrums, and by enduring them and understanding their causes she can turn a troubled, fearful child into a calm, affectionate one. By showing them she cares, Corinne gets the children to respond in kind. They want to work for her because they know she loves them."

The different qualities in these two ordinary people, thrown together in a most unusual place where there were no rules, no road map, no real plans, proved an extraordinary combination and made for a chemistry that would allow them to not only form but also realize their dreams. We can never know, even with reading Bob's frank and insightful *A Flock of Lambs*, the precise chemistry between them. We can only observe its manifestations and marvel at their shared desire to better the lives of mentally disabled people.

But it would be wrong to think of them only as altruists; they were also visionaries and innovators, certainly.

1976

Dorm construction completed; First Lady Betty Ford dedicates building on March 12

Dr. Karl Menninger visits

Decades after she had left the Bonaparte School, Corinne said, "Our young people love to be useful but hate to be used," and looking at her then, one could not help but see a grandmotherly image. Bob, after knowing her for 30 years, said that he had never seen her hurt anyone. Unsworth, in *The Lambs of Libertyville*, wrote that "behind the self-effacing exterior, there is a master teacher."

The authorship of *A Flock of Lambs* is credited to Bob Terese "with" Corinne Owen, and its dedication reads: "To the mentally retarded, our good and dear friends, who give us more love every twenty-four hours than most human beings receive in a lifetime."

I like to think that the answer to what motivated these two people, or at least part of it, is in those words, simple as they may be. And that answer is love.

"We didn't know what we were doing.
We just knew our people. The merest hint
of a 'them and us' attitude will do more
to destroy what you are trying to build than
anything you can think of."

BONAPARTE SCHOOL

The Bonaparte School was built in 1910. It was a classic one-room schoolhouse in the Chicago suburb of Glen Ellyn when much of the surrounding area was farmland. With increased population there came the need for bigger and newer schools, and in 1950 Bonaparte was closed. It sat forlornly on a slight rise behind the grounds of the Morton Arboretum awaiting a wrecking ball.

Two years later, anyone driving by the school would have been surprised to see it filled with activity. People were inside scrubbing it clean and outside giving it a new coat of paint. These were members of Community Welfare for Mentally Retarded Children, part of a statewide group that was fighting for state-financed instruction for mentally disabled children. A recently introduced bill for that funding had been defeated in the latest session of the Illinois Legislature, so these people had set out to do something on their own.

This was one of many similar efforts that had begun to dot the Chicago area. There were no provisions at boards of education for training or educating retarded children. Those parents who were unwilling to place their children in public-run institutions and unable to afford the few private schools available for the mentally disabled, yet were reluctant to keep them shuttered away at home, had no choice but to open their own schools out of frustration and need.

"In the late 1950s, the mentally retarded were among the most scorned, isolated, and neglected groups in American society.

The Lambs Institute is established

First Tennis Ball is held for $50 per ticket

Carol Burnett visits

Mental retardation was viewed as a hopeless, shameful disease, and those afflicted with it were shunned from sight as soon as possible," Edward Shorter wrote in his book *The Kennedy Family and the Story of Mental Retardation.*

The practices of the time are almost unimaginable now. Some parents shipped their children off to institutions characterized by more than one observer as hellholes and, as Shorter put it, "unspeakable traps for forgotten people—living in a state of squalor and deprivation." Some of the parents who sent their children away published fake death notices in local papers, and some held mock funerals including tiny coffins filled with nothing but the parents' shame and guilt. Nobel Prize-winning author Pearl Buck, the mother of a mentally disabled child, said in 1950, "Parents of retarded children could only welcome the death of their afflicted offspring."

Thirty-seven young people, ages six to 22, were registered to attend Bonaparte School. They lived in Glen Ellyn and surrounding suburbs. They were instructed by a single hired teacher and

1978

Mr. and Mrs.
Gaylord Donnelley
receive the Good
Shepherd Award

The Lambs
Institute, founded
to offer conferences,
workshops and
seminars for
professionals, parents
and others, joins the
Chicago Consortium
of Colleges and
Universities

mothers volunteering their time. The school day was from 9 a.m. to 5 p.m. Monday through Friday. Tuition was $5 a week.

The remade school contained two rooms on the main floor and, in the basement, a small room and a kitchen. As Bob Terese noted, it "was not air-, water-, or animal-tight. Wind and rain were frequent visitors, as well as an occasional gopher or mouse. At times it seemed that the country itself was trying to reclaim the school."

At Bonaparte, Bob and Corinne began working in tandem to develop and put into action the ideas that would form the basis of their mission. They divided their students by abilities, broke down tasks into easy steps, and worked on students' social skills and the sorts of tasks, like playing store, that they saw as meaningful. They also taught the students silkscreening and basic cooking. Bob later said of their methods, "We didn't know what the hell we were doing." Corinne added, "We just knew our people."

To get our young people to trust themselves, to like themselves, to be able to rely upon themselves; this was—and is—one of our greatest tasks at The Lambs.

1978

1979

Carol Burnett returns to become an Honorary Board member

Kresge Challenge Grant is received for Restaurant ground breaking

Construction begins on Group Homes; "Teaching the Mentally Retarded" booklet is completed by Corinne Owen

There was a wonderful freedom in that, and those who considered their methods unconventional—and many did—should have known that there were no conventions. Another sad statistic of the time: In 1957, at all universities in the United States, there were only 28 instructors working full-time to prepare teachers to work with the mentally disabled.

From the Bonaparte School, Bob and Corinne went on, separately but within months of one another, to work at Hull House's Retarded Children's Aid. There they were dismayed to find that students were tied to the drudgery of repetitive chores— unimaginative tasks such as fitting nuts and bolts together and packaging them or sticking a predetermined number of hairpins on a square of cardboard.

This did not sit well with Bob and Corinne. "We wanted to give these people dignity, self-confidence, a purpose; to discover their potential and make them productive, independent, well-rounded individuals; to increase the quality of their lives," she said.

1980

Waukegan residence opens; Group Homes open; former Governor Dan Walker plays in 3RD annual Tennis Ball

Nine Group Homes are built through a $2.6 million, 40 year loan from the U.S. Department of Housing and Urban Development

First Lady Betty Ford cuts the ribbon at the Grand Opening of the Country Inn Restaurant

They began taking the children on field trips, started cooking classes with them, and had them paint their own classrooms. They began to think about starting a business, and they shared that idea with parents and with Hull House. Many of the parents loved the idea. Administrators did not.

In 1960, two weeks before Christmas, Bob and Corinne were fired.

We'll call it The Lambs, from the biblical passage in which Christ tells his disciples to 'Feed my lambs.'—Bob Terese

THE PET STORE

Twelve sets of parents each contributed $50 toward the rent of a storefront on State Street, not far from Holy Name Cathedral, the swinging Rush Street nightclub area, the Water Tower, which had survived the Chicago Fire, and the expensive homes of the Gold Coast and Streeterville.

The space was a mess, its floor covered with debris and the walls flaked down to the brickwork. Toilets were cracked, and there was a hole in the roof where an air conditioner once hummed. It had previously been home to a Magikist Rug Cleaners outlet, and the landlord demanded the same $325 a month that Magikist had been paying. Bob and Corinne did not have that kind of money.

They, of so much faith, arranged a meeting with William Gage, the president of Magikist, which still held the lease on the State Street space. Gage later recalled for a magazine journalist, "I get hundreds of requests for contributions. Bob and Corinne were so honest and sincere. They were only helping a few—12 kids—and they had a thousand things to do."

Gage agreed to pay the rent on the space for six months, saying, "They didn't know what they'd do with the money I'd saved them—but that's why I gave it to them. They needed it so badly."

The sincerity and honesty that Gage felt had an effect on many others. The president of Pioneer Pet Supply, L. Clifford Gardner, donated $8,000 worth of supplies and put the arm on others to do likewise. Jewel Tea Company gave movable shelves, and the decorating department of the Fair Department Store helped

Dear World :
I love
The Lambs. They
do a wonderful job!
Ann Landers

1981

1982

The Vocational Work Center opens and employs residents in subcontracted jobs; the Women's Board Wall of Love is established

The Lambs Skills Component Program begins offering residents classes on daily living skills; the Pet Shop undergoes major renovation

James S. Kemper, Jr. receives the Good Shepherd Award; Joseph Regenstein, Jr. receives the Good Shepherd Award; Ann Landers attends the event

design the 600-square-foot space. A contractor donated new heating and plumbing equipment. Lighting fixtures, bird cages, and almost everything else in the store was donated.

It opened on September 28, 1961. Punch and cookies were served. A television crew showed up, as did a reporter from the *Chicago Tribune.*

"Do your people here appreciate what has been done?" the reporter asked Bob.

"Like all children, you give them a gift and they don't ask where it came from," he replied.

The reporter noted the store's "bright and cheery décor" and called it a "pioneering venture for the mentally retarded." He saw a large plate glass window fronting the street and shaded by a green and yellow awning, a main room of bright red awnings overhanging shelves, and a back wall painted with animal figures, as well as 20 tanks of tropical fish, cages filled with parakeets and canaries, six hamsters, and a raccoon named Sweetie.

Before the day is over, always assure the young persons that you still love them, care for them, and need them. Make sure they know that you do not expect a repetition of the inappropriate behavior, but that tomorrow is a new day and the slate will be rubbed clean.

	1986		1988

The Country Kitchen opens and more than doubles the production facility

Sweet Street. the Ice Cream Parlor and Pastry Shop, opens for business; The Lambs acquires 12 acres of adjacent property for future growth

The Lambs celebrates 25 years of dedicated service to the mentally retarded; Robert G. Haas Athletic Field is dedicated

The television show "20/20" features Lambs Farm

The reporter asked about the origin of the store's name and learned that it had come in a flash of inspiration one day when Bob picked Corinne up in his car.

"We'll call it The Lambs," Bob said.

Corinne knew its origin, the biblical passage in which Christ tells his disciples to "feed my lambs."

"It's perfect," she said.

Those who came on the store's opening day were impressed. Bob, Corinne, and the employees were pleased. But no one was aware that on this day The Lambs became the first nonsheltered business employing mentally disabled young adults in the United States.

And business was good.

There were many stories in the newspapers and on television. U.S. Senator Adlai Stevenson of Illinois, his wife, Nancy, and their children came in almost weekly. Members of the prominent Wrigley and Pritzker families shopped at the store. A Playboy bunny or two came in to ogle the birds (the mansion and club were nearby), as did one notable local mobster.

By the winter of 1965, the number of children working in the store had risen from 12 to 20; some of them had also begun to work at the Carson Pirie Scott & Company department store downtown; and the operation had managed to put $25,000 in the bank. "All the signs pointed to our branching out," Bob wrote. "In the evolution of our plans, our thoughts first centered on only one or the other of our needs—new activity or home. [In 1965] the two finally came together."

"I think we saw it as an ideal society," Corinne Owen said. "We believed we could create an ideal society, one that would offer a workday, something to come home to, and a full social life. We could be a model not only for mental retardation but for institutions that are housing the blind or the physically handicapped or the aged."

THE FARM

W. Clement Stone—self-made millionaire, Chicago philanthropist, and self-help book author soon to depart on a three-month European vacation—was sitting in his office when Julie Ann Lyman called. She wanted to see him, and because she had recently written a flattering profile of him for the *Tribune*, he agreed to give her 10 minutes the next morning.

"We've got ourselves a farm."—Bob Terese

Corinne and Bob share their dream of a renovated barn to house the pet shop with W. Clement Stone, Chicago philanthropist, and Joseph Meek, president of the Illinois Retailers Association.

The details of the actual conversation between Lyman and Stone are lost to history, but the result was of everlasting impact. Lyman called Bob immediately after her meeting with Stone, and Bob called Corinne.

"Corinne," he said. "We've got ourselves a farm."

It had not been easy. When Bob and Corinne first saw the property, they thought it would be perfect. "We felt that the farm, the potential inherent in its land and buildings, coincided almost exactly with our philosophy of working with the retarded," Bob wrote. "But the main reason behind our great desire to acquire the farm was that, once our home was built, that home and that farm would always be there. No one would need to fear any longer, neither the young people nor their parents, what would happen to them. There would always be somewhere warm and loving for them to go."

There was just one problem, and it was a major one: The asking price for the property was $186,000.

They were able to persuade the owners of the property to give them a three-month option for $1, and then they tried to raise the rest of the money. Although one of the parents in the program was wealthy, Bob said, "he was not *that* wealthy"; some executives of a large pet-food business listened politely to their pitch before even more politely rebuffing them. June 1965 became July, and July became August; and three days before the deadline they shared their worries with Lyman, who had written a lovely story about the pet shop.

> "Corinne and I felt that the farm, the potential inherent in its land and buildings, coincided almost exactly with our philosophy."

1989			1990

Construction of Founders Building begins; Miniature golf course opens

Corinne Owen and Bob Terese receive the Good Shepherd Award; Mike Ditka is keynote speaker; the Pet Shop is renovated

Small Animal Nursery opens with assistance from Dr. Lester Fisher; miniature train and golf driving range opens; Vocational Work Center moves to Lake Bluff site

Lyman saw Stone, and he agreed to buy the property. The Lambs paid him the same amount they were paying for rent on their State Street store.

It was a lovely piece of land, 50 acres near the northwest suburb of Libertyville that contained the largest stone barn in the state, two farmhouses, and a 15-acre lake. But like the State Street

Artist's rendering of a residence that would result in nine 12-person Group Homes.

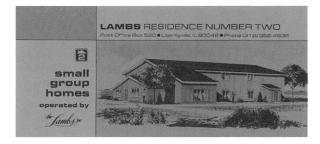

1990

Tim Unsworth writes "The Lambs of Libertyville"; Founders Building construction is completed

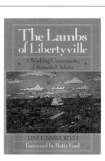

1991

Silkscreen shop expands; Country Inn Restaurant is redecorated with assistance from P. Buckley Moss

"Fabulous Fare" cookbook is published by the Women's Board

store before they moved in, the farm and its buildings needed work. Corinne saw its potential, however: "We saw it as an ideal society. We believed we could create an ideal society, one that would offer a workday, something to come home to, and a full social life. We could be a model not only for mental retardation but for institutions that are housing the blind or the physically handicapped or the aged."

"The Lambs provides a unique and deeply caring program which has touched and changed hundreds of lives. You have my sincere congratulations for the work you do. Through the training and career opportunities provided, the Lambs enables special people to live independent lives."—First Lady Betty Ford

Corinne with First Lady Betty Ford at the Grand Opening of the Dorm in 1976.

Bob and Corinne and many volunteers worked hard to reclaim the land, to repair its buildings, and to quickly open another pet store and start a vegetable stand. In time they added a restaurant, a farmer's market, a bakery, and a petting zoo. In a decade there would be a ribbon cutting—signifying the realization of a long-standing dream—for the first residence at the farm and the opening of a new restaurant, more residences, and a thrift store.

Stone eventually gave the property to The Lambs; and then it became known as Lambs Farm. Famous people would come to visit—First Lady Betty Ford cut the ribbon—as did sociologists, psychologists, and others in the field from more than 50 countries, as well as hundreds of thousands of less well known people, most simply seeking a day in the country.

A few decades after the opening of The Lambs, Corinne said, "Our people are so very special because they love you all the time. They don't see anything wrong with you. They don't know how to tell a lie. Some people think they would become depressed if they came for a visit. On the contrary, everyone who comes has a positive experience and leaves with a much better understanding of the mentally retarded. It is a happy outing."

"What we wanted to accomplish was to give the adult retarded a sense of accomplishment, a sense of performance," Bob Terese said. "But more important than that, we were taking the fear out of life—and fear is the most crippling handicap to those with disabilities as well as those without."

FIONA

She wanted to see a goat—and a father wants to make his daughter happy.

"Daddy, do they have goats there?" she asked.

Her name is Fiona Kogan; she is my six-year-old daughter, and on a windy and sun-splashed day in early April this year she made her first trip to Lambs Farm. She is a city child, and as such is more familiar with cabs than cows. We urban dwellers are long and far removed from farm life. And so, Fiona and I spent the day at the farm.

She was curious about everything—she is six after all—and so she wanted to know the names of all the animals she petted. After a couple of hours she asked, "Who made this neat place?"

It has been more than a decade since Bob and Corinne walked this land. They both died in 1999, he of a heart attack in January and she of a blood clot in her brain that December. By then they had seen so many of their dreams realized. They had received all manner of awards and praise. They had watched the world change for mentally disabled people and knew they had helped make that happen. They would be happy to see how The Lambs has continued to thrive in the years since their deaths.

And as Fiona and I walked close to the shores of the lake, she asked, "Do people live here?"

I thought of a boy in the Old Town neighborhood in which I grew up whose name was Joe and who was, I now know, mentally disabled. He was kept at home, just down the street from where

1992	1993	1994	1995
Brunswick donates pontoon boat	Mr. and Mrs. Jack Galter receive the Good Shepherd Award; Carousel added to attractions	The Flying Elvi are the featured attraction at the Elvis Country Fair Day	Construction begins on Benjamin B. Green-Field Residence; Appley House opens (Libertyville residence)

I lived, and we would see him sometimes on summer days, staring out the window as we played football, baseball, and other games in the street in front of his house. He always looked sad. Then one day, he was no longer in the window, and we wondered where he had gone. But we didn't ask—we just went about our games and our growing up.

The past does, as it should, echo through the years. So, Fiona and I had breakfast (we shared a waffle) and a late lunch (we shared a cheeseburger) at the farm, and for both meals a very nice young man brought us silverware and water. The restaurant was not very crowded, so he stood close to our table, vigilant.

"I am happy to see you again," he said when we came in for lunch. "You must be very hungry to come here twice in one day."

"I am," said Fiona. "But I don't want another waffle."

"The cheeseburgers are very good," he said. "Do you want one of those?"

She did.

1996		1999
Michael Kurschner wins bronze medal at World Special Olympics Games in New Haven, Connecticut; actor Chris Burke (Corky from "Life Goes On") visits Lambs Farm	6.7 acres of additional land are acquired; Benjamin B. Green-Field Residence opens	Co-founders Corinne Owen and Bob Terese pass away

"Do you like movies?" he asked her while she ate. "I liked *Tangled.*"

"Me too," said Fiona, her bright eyes growing brighter. "Did you like best the part where…?"

For a few minutes they talked about the film, sharing laughs about their favorite scenes and characters. As I listened to them, I could hear Bob's voice: "The greatest obstacle to a retarded child's adjustment to the normal world is fear." And hearing that, I realized that the greatest obstacle to the normal person's adjustment to the mentally disabled world is also fear.

And Bob's voice again: "The unique thing about The Lambs is that it is open to the public. It's exciting. I'm delighted we get so many young kids here. It helps clear up misconceptions when kids are very young."

I wanted to tell Fiona that before The Lambs came into being, people like the person she was talking to and laughing with would have been people she might never have met, people who,

Over the years, Bob Terese and Corinne Owen had taught a huge urban and suburban community that fear is a great barrier to society.

2002	2003	2004
Groundbreaking ceremony takes place for W. Clement and Jessie V. Stone Apartments	Corinne Owen House opens (Mundelein residence); Hill House opens (Waukegan residence); Group Home renovation project is initiated	High Rollers basketball team wins first place in senior division of Special Olympics

a half century ago, were deemed incapable of development, bereft of essential humanity.

That's a bit much for a six-year-old, so I said instead, "It's time to go." As we walked toward the door, she said, "I forgot something," and I watched as she went back to the young man and gave him a hug.

That day and its encounters and observations and memories may not change Fiona's life in any obvious ways. I know—hope—that she is going to grow up in a world in which certain inequities of the past have been erased, a place that is more accepting, more tolerant, more enlightened. Kinder.

Fiona never knew my father. He died long before she was born. And my mother was infirm in body and mind when Fiona was born and died before she was two. She is ever curious about the grandparents she would never know, so I told her a story about her grandmother while we wandered through the Lambs gift store. It is a story my mother never told me but that I discovered in rereading *A Flock of Lambs*. There was so much in the book that I had forgotten.

2008	2009	2010	2011
Popcorn Days fundraising event is initiated	Golf Day celebrates its 25TH anniversary	Lambs Farm is awarded three-year accreditation from the Commission on Accreditation of Rehabilitation Facilities with a perfect survey	

The Terese family attends Friends of the Farm Day

Near its end Bob wrote, "We opened the gift shop at the same time we did the dining room, and it would have been a very empty shop indeed without the generosity of Marilew Kogan. She was doing some public relations work for us at the time and donated three months of her salary to buying our first gift shop items."

"Grandma Marilew bought all of these things?" Fiona asked.

"Not all of them," I said.

On our way out of the farm, Fiona wanted to make one last stop. We walked into the pet store again, toward the cages filled with yapping puppies. I could once more hear the sound of yapping puppies in a pet shop on State Street long ago. I began to think of the amazing thing that is the circle of life and realized that all people should be allowed to be part of it. And I was happy that at this farm, on this day, Fiona and I were, and so were all the people we met.

Like all of us, Fiona will learn with time that life is not fair. But some days it seems just fine.

"This is Mayberry, U.S.A.," one long-term employee said of the community at the farm. She was exaggerating, but there is a kind of bucolic, ambling pace about the neighborhood that is infectious. One only has to make eye contact, and one will be greeted. Just as important, the visitor will be remembered.

It is often said that life is what you make of it. Each of us determines what will make our lives personally fulfilling through our different experiences, opportunities, and hopes for the future. Despite these differences, we all want and deserve those things that are at the heart of a satisfying life—a safe, comfortable home, a meaningful job, health and well-being, enriching experiences, social activities with friends, and the spirit of family and community. At Lambs Farm, these facets of a fulfilling life are embraced every day. Whether it is gaining independence by moving into a new home or acquiring the skills and confidence necessary to join the workforce, each of the men and women we serve is defining and achieving his or her personal life goals, and seizing every opportunity to savor all the things life is made of—home, work, recreation, friendships and enriching experiences.

Lambs Farm Today

HOME AND FAMILY

When you think of home, the words comfort, safety, and togetherness readily come to mind. Our Participants have a variety of residential options that offer these things, all with different levels of staff support, physical and medical assistance, and independence to meet their personal needs.

In their daily lives, our residents experience a sense of home by preparing and eating meals side by side, relaxing in the evenings together, and sharing the concerns and responsibilities of a household.

The Declaration of Independence promises life, liberty, and the pursuit of happiness. At Lambs Farm, each life is blossoming with opportunities for independence, and Participants embrace that independence to make their own choices every day—where to live, which jobs to pursue, whether to play sports, and with whom to socialize.

Similar to an experienced farmer nurturing his crops from spring through fall, Lambs Farm delights in the Participants' emerging independence. Some are at the seedling stage, developing their self-care skills; others are ready to harvest, preparing their own meals and maintaining their own apartments. At every step of the way, there are chances to explore what each person wants for his or her own life experience. They know they must sow their life skills first so that they may soon reap the benefits of independence.

A waiting list of more than 200 men and women
with developmental disabilities holds the future
for themselves and their families. For those
on the list, it is the realization of a dream as they
wait for the opportunity to live a more independent
life with their peers. For their families, it is the
culmination of a lifetime of caregiving and the end
of fear for who will take care of their loved one if
something happens to them. When the time finally
comes, it is a bittersweet moment for all.

After the move to Lambs Farm, families often express that their loved one has "really blossomed" and grown in their independence and decision-making skills.

WORK

The men and women of Lambs Farm can choose from an array of options available to learn vocational skills and experience meaningful employment in one of our campus businesses or in the community. When it comes to finding a job, our Career Services Center serves as an employment office where information on employment opportunities, training classes, and vocational counseling is readily available. As they hone valuable skills at their jobs, our Participants achieve an important element of personal fulfillment—the confidence and pride that come with being successful in the workplace.

Our founding business, Lambs Pet Shop, serves as one of our vocational training sites on campus where Participants learn skills in store maintenance, animal care, and interaction with customers. The unconditional and nonjudgmental love they feel from the animals is like none other.

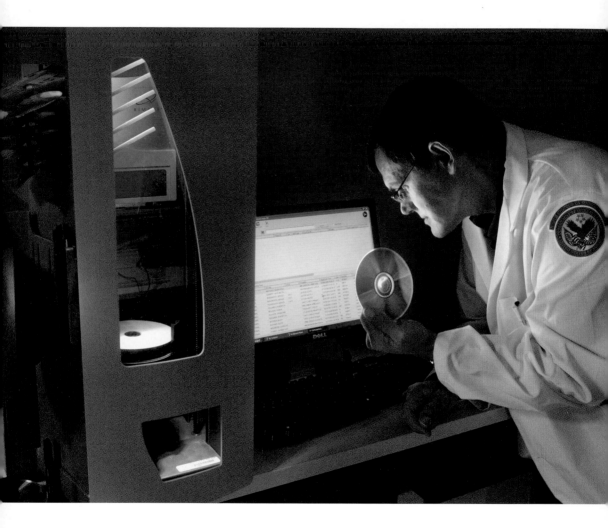

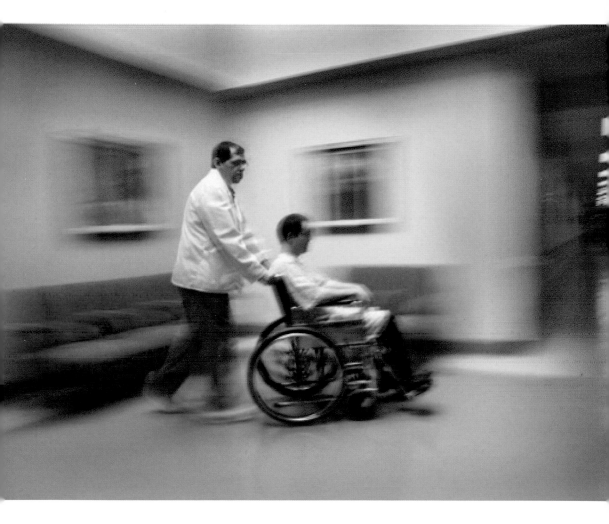

Many of our Participants enjoy careers in the community, working
many years for the same employer, and holding responsible jobs as respected
members of the workforce.

Independent. Excited. Responsible. Those are the words that describe

how Participants feel when they are able to complete something on their

own. Through enthusiasm and determination to learn new skills, the respect

of co-workers is earned and the depth of potential recognized. Participants

in the Employment Services Program define their character by applying

their abilities to meaningful work, facing new challenges, and continually

uncovering new achievements.

A first impression is rarely forgotten. The Participants of Lambs Farm
are often the first faces to greet visitors. Many discover their niche and their
gift for speaking with others. Visitors are impressed with their knowledge
of the organization and are often charmed by their humor, personality, and
exemplary customer service. Participants want customers to leave with
a happy smile and a good attitude. Yet they always leave with something
more—a lasting memory of their experience.

With enthusiasm and determination, Participants of Lambs Farm become true team members of the staff, taking pride in their work and feeling a great sense of accomplishment.

Meaningful employment imparts a feeling of importance, responsibility,

teamwork, and confidence—all things that help people grow into themselves.

Nowhere is that more important than at Lambs Farm. Participants rise

in the morning with the sun and ready themselves for the day of work ahead.

Some make their way to the bakery where they produce Lambs Farm's

famous butter cookies, homemade granola, and even treats for dogs.

No matter the job, new skills and life lessons are learned every day,

as Participants gain confidence and pride in their work and themselves.

That desire to gain new skills and expand abilities is a human drive, one that

is extremely strong and encouraged among the people of Lambs Farm.

Independence comes in many forms. Some Participants still living at home with family enjoy the freedom of their commute to work on campus at one of our vocational work sites.

The Thrift Shop, started in 1980 by the Women's Board, provides a rewarding experience for both Participants and customers alike.

Participants enjoy the variety of jobs at Lambs Industries where they specialize in subcontract jobs such as assembly, packaging, sorting and mailing services.

RECREATION AND HEALTH

Just as the summer rain replenishes a parched landscape, Lambs Farm's recreation programs rejuvenate Participants throughout the year. Physical fitness, Special Olympics, and healthy lifestyle activities are an important part of their daily lives. They play an active role in maintaining and improving health and well-being. Participants can work toward achieving their nutrition and fitness goals by joining the Healthy Lambs Program where regular exercise is monitored and rewarded, or by taking a HealthWise class to learn proper eating habits and meal preparation.

Lambs Lake is a calm, peaceful body of water surrounded by wooded banks and campus Group Homes that are home to over 100 residents. Curved pathways frame the east side of the lake, which is used for recreation and as a place for relaxation and meditation.

Feeling the wind blow through their hair as they pedal a three-wheeled bike around the outdoor track doesn't seem like exercise to Participants, but while laughing with friends they are strengthening muscles and increasing

heart health. Others meet regularly in the weight room to compare strength and endurance. This competition between friends shows that exercise doesn't have to be boring. The dedication of Participants to making sound choices for a productive life proves an inspiration and sets an example that everyone could follow.

Engaging in hobbies and pursuing personal interests are fostered.
One personal interest is expressed through a connection with all things
equestrian.

Many Participants take part in recreational activities such as basketball, track and field, tennis, and swimming. They experience the dynamics of regular exercise combined with the camaraderie of a team effort by training in nine Special Olympics sports.

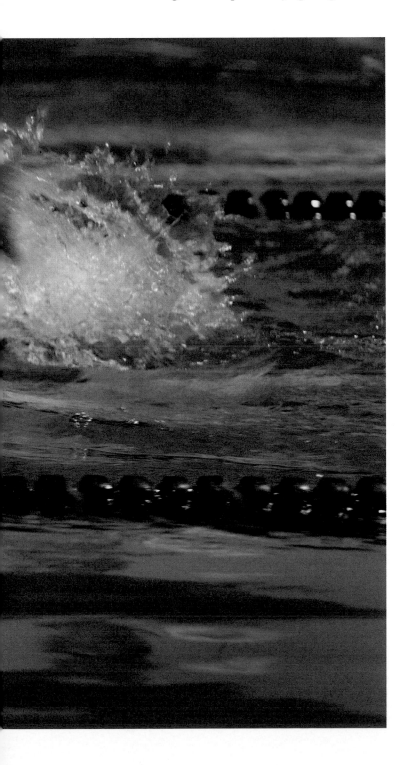

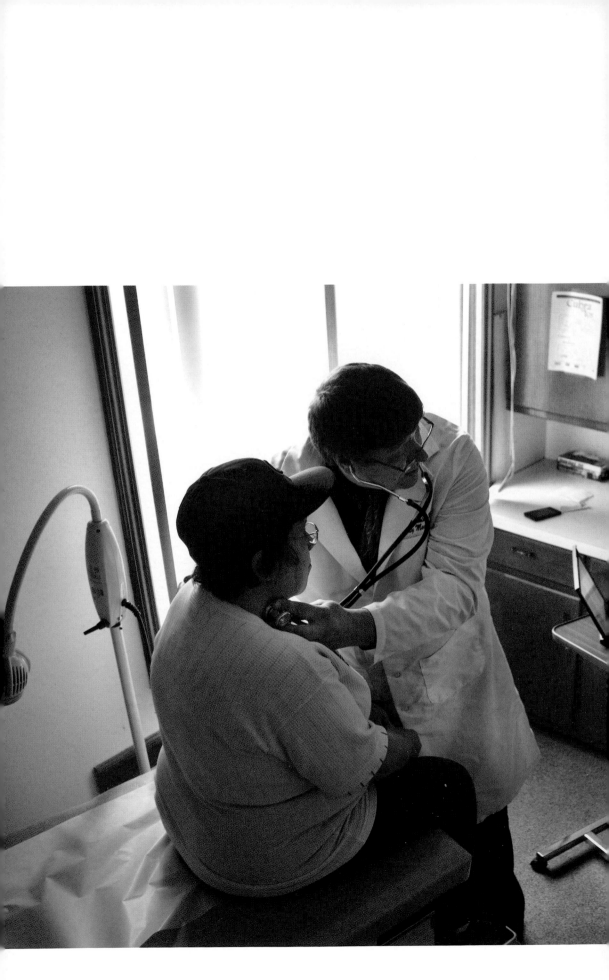

Maintaining good health is a top priority. Whether it is a visit to a nurse in our Health Services department, or a regular appointment with a doctor in the community or one of the many specialists who regularly visit our campus, Participants want to be as fit as possible. Certainly, they do not want an illness to interfere with their busy lifestyles.

ENRICHMENT

A bountiful harvest is dependent on a steady
flow of water and good fertilizer. Education and
varied activities give Lambs Farm Participants the
confidence to reach beyond themselves and grow,
exploring the world around them through a
wide range of experiences including job training,
Quest classes, outings, and trips to cultural venues.
As we interact with others, we impart our
unique knowledge and expand our own horizons.
The people of Lambs Farm do not simply learn
from those they meet, they also teach us—
that although we are all different on the outside,
it is the human spirit we share that nourishes us.

Engaging in creative pursuits can help individuals see the world in a
new way. Programs such as Quest, a voluntary enrichment program with
some 200 classes annually on topics recommended by a committee of
Participants, help class members gain important life skills and allow

individuals to express themselves creatively through classes such
as Photography and Poetry. The members of the Quest photography class
do more than just take pictures; through photography they connect
with each other, their families, the things they love, their pain, and the
world in which they live. The class also unveils a world of curiosity
and limitless possibilities.

The simple pleasure of reading a good book is not taken for granted
at Lambs Farm. Some Participants who were denied an education now
revel in the enjoyment of words that lead into a sentence. Others
get to enjoy the local library's bookmobile and share their favorite books
and movies with their friends.

For our artists at heart, nothing brings the promise of unbridled creativity like colored pencils or a rainbow of paints. They are able to retreat to a world where bright colors such as yellow, red, and blue burst, and pastels such as blush and mint green whisper softly. It is a place to engage the creative process and the human spirit—a place of freedom and imagination.

Lambs Farm Participants are given opportunities to explore their
natural talents and to pursue interests they find enjoyable. The array
of options available is exceeded only by the number of ways Participants
take advantage of them.

FRIENDSHIP AND LEISURE TIME

The lasting friendships with co-workers, housemates, and staff are
yet another network of support available to Participants. Sharing
experiences, learning, laughing, and quibbling and reconciling with peers
all contribute to living a life of independence. Within Lambs Farm
there is a strong sense of pride and community. Participants pay visits to
each others' houses, work, cook, travel, enjoy sports, and care for one
another. These collective experiences destroy the antiquated notion that
being different means being excluded.

Spending time with peers generates feelings of comfort and contentment, and a sense of belonging. Participants at Lambs Farm socialize together spreading the news of the day, sharing their own daily experiences in the comfort of one another's company while enjoying laughs along the way.

The men and women of Lambs Farm have an enthusiasm for life that
is evident as they pursue lifelong interests and hobbies, form friendships,
and spend time with their peers. Monthly parties and dances provide
opportunities to enjoy each other's company and have fun. Making
lifelong friends is easy at Lambs Farm. The warm, family environment
attracts those wishing to spend time together. Good advice and
companionship are never more than a few feet away.

COMMUNITY

As integral members of the towns surrounding the campus, residents regularly
go into these communities for shopping, banking, errands, or recreation.
Participants may also choose to join group outings to sporting events, musicals,
dinners, and more or use our regularly scheduled Rainbow Run to visit area
stores, libraries, theaters, or restaurants. Whether taking part in local events

and activities, visiting area attractions, relaxing in the parks, or shopping,

our Participants fully enjoy all of the amenities of their local communities.

Welcoming the general public to our campus businesses and events also

creates opportunities for Participants to interact with their fellow citizens

from surrounding communities.

Because of their diverse interests and beliefs, Participants often pursue an interest in spirituality. Some join Christian church groups, some practice Jewish traditions, and others choose to follow a more personal set of beliefs. As adults living independent lives, support from community religious organizations helps many Participants deal with life's complex issues. Friends travel together on both Saturdays and Sundays to various houses of worship, seeking advice, comfort, and solace. For some God is in the sky; for others God is in a smile or in the welcoming arms of friends and family.

As productive members of society, Lambs Farm Participants can be found volunteering for other organizations, working for community employers, and living in nearby neighborhoods. Many volunteer at local churches, long-term care facilities, and other organizations. Others find camaraderie through membership in community groups.

Volunteers are the backbone of most nonprofit organizations, and Lambs Farm is no exception. Lambs Farm benefits from the dedicated services of extraordinary individuals. Whether volunteers are teaching Quest classes for Participants, providing technology assistance, painting buildings, coaching Special Olympics athletes, sorting Thrift Shop donations, or playing one of the many other vital roles so important to fulfilling the Lambs Farm mission, they deserve grateful thanks and appreciation.

**"That we have been so successful is the result of
the efforts of all our good, kind friends. Corinne and
I could never have brought about either the State Street
store or the farm on our own. And yet, now that
The Lambs is a success, we also know that it can continue
to succeed only if we keep it simple. "—Bob Terese**

This book ends, but our story goes on...

EPILOGUE

It was a simple idea: that there had to be something better for their "young people" than was being offered in 1961—that given the opportunity, people with developmental disabilities could become productive members of society.

Today, Lambs Farm is a place that provides all of the essential ingredients for people to grow: a safe, caring, living environment; an extended family of peers with shared values and mutual respect; and opportunities to have productive employment and to make a contribution to the community while being as self-sufficient as possible.

It is rooted in the belief that all people are valuable and that, given the right conditions, all can lead more productive, fulfilling, and happy lives. Lambs Farm believes that the human spirit needs more than just physical nourishment to survive, and that social interaction and productive work are equally essential.

To our residents, Lambs Farm is home, and a place they are proud to share with our visitors. To our visitors, Lambs Farm is a place to grow through enriching experiences with people with developmental disabilities while also creating lasting connections between their families and ours.

Lambs Farm is about helping people, and allowing those people the self-respect and dignity gained from helping themselves. It is about self-reliance, hard work, and a nurturing environment, all coming together to cultivate human fulfillment. Lambs Farm is a place where all people grow.

Acknowledgments

Lambs Farm would not exist were it not for all of those who came before us. They not only built the foundation upon which this remarkable organization has grown, but left a legacy of compassion, dedication and commitment that will carry into the future.

This book would not have been possible without the contributions of literally hundreds of people. In particular, Kathy Buresch, whose penchant for perfection consumed untold hours of diligent copy review and the writing and editing of the words that accompany the photos; Jackie Rachev, for her patience in scheduling the numerous photo shoots; and, of course, Bob Feie, whose design genius brought all facets together in striking fashion.

Most of all, we are grateful for the inspiration of the men and women of Lambs Farm, who set an example for all of us by facing each daily challenge with courage and enthusiasm, and cherishing the opportunity to live life to the fullest.